the king's singers

Book of Rounds, Canons and Partsongs

ISBN 0-634-04630-6

the colour of song

EXCLUSIVELY DISTRIBUTED BY

HAL•LEONARD®
CORPORATION
7777 W. BLUEMOUND RD. P.O. BOX 13819 MILWAUKEE, WI 53213

Visit Hal Leonard Online at
www.halleonard.com

CONTENTS

English Pre-1700 (Secular)

Pre-1700 (Sacred)

Post-1700

From Around the World

Wordless Rounds

INTRODUCTION

The round must be one of the earliest forms of multi-voice vocal music, since it was already well-established in the Elizabethan period as a kind of poor musician's madrigal. It is a simple form of canon – a canon at the unison. "Canon" means "rule" and the rule is that one part sings a tune and is imitated by other parts joining in one by one. Some canons, even those from the earliest times, display great ingenuity by having the voices imitate not at the unison but at other tones of the scale, imitating with longer notes, shorter notes, even upside down or backwards.

This collection contains many examples, both sacred and secular, from the very early but extraordinarily forward-looking "Summer Is A-Coming In," the extensive works of Thomas Ravenscroft, some later and less well-known canons and rounds of the Romantic period, to the ingenious partsong by John Stainer, which can actually be read upside down to produce another partsong.

So why rounds and canons? This is hardly King's Singers repertoire. Fair enough, only a handful of the numbers would appear in a typical King's Singers concert. But for once, the motivation was not the desire to share some of our music with the choral fraternity (and sorority!) in an attempt to accommodate the many requests we get to release our repertoire for general consumption.

Two of the elements which govern our approach to ensemble singing, blend and balance, are properly achieved only through listening while singing. What better way to encourage listening than a form which is simple melodically (allowing the mind to focus in other directions) but which when put together produces ready-made and sometimes complex harmony, and in the case of the round, offers the almost unique opportunity (that is to say excepting unison music such as plainsong) to work on music where the raw materials for the production of perfect blend and balance are identical in every part?

We have deliberately left out tempo and dynamic indications, so that you can choose your own. It might even be a good idea to practice the pieces at different speeds on different days, using various dynamic levels, always aiming to increase your choir's range of vocal colours, and keep the singers on their toes! You may also want to transpose up or down as you feel necessary. The point where each new voice starts is indicated and, in some cases, the point where each stops (with a fermata), but whether they all stop at the same time, or the last voice to enter is allowed to run its course, and how many times the piece "goes round" – all this is for you to decide. The beauty of this collection is that it is highly varied and flexible, and we hope it will be a useful tool for choir directors, not for creating a concert programme, but for exercising the singers, expanding the colour palette of the choir, and above all, encouraging listening by every single member.

Finally, a word of thanks. We are heavily indebted to Emily Crocker, Vice President of Choral Publications at Hal Leonard, for much valuable help with research, and to Dan Stolper, Choral Editor, for his usual tireless efforts in co-ordinating layout, presentation and proof reading.

We all hope you have as much fun using this collection as we had compiling it.

The King's Singers

1. ADIEU, SWEET AMARILLIS

Anonymous

A - dieu, sweet A - ma - ril - lis, for since to part, your

O heav - y _____ tid -

Yet once a - gain, ere that I

will is, A - dieu, sweet A - ma - ril - lis. *(to ②)*

- ing, there is for me no bid - ing. *(to ③)*

part with you, A - ma - ril - lis sweet, _ a - dieu. *(to ①)*

2. AH, POOR BIRD

English

Ah, poor bird, take thy flight,

Far a - bove the shad - ows of this sad night.

3. AH, ROBYN, GENTIL ROBYN

William Cornysh (d. 1523)

Part I

Ah, Rob - yn, gen - til Rob - yn, tell me how thy

Part I

le - man doth and thow shalt know of myne. A Rob - yn, gen - til Rob

Part II

A Rob - yn, gen - til Rob

yn, tell me how thy le-man doth and thow shalt know of myne.

yn, tell me how thy le - man doth and thow shalt know of myne.

Part I

A Rob - yn, gen - til Rob - yn, tell me how thy le - man doth and

Part II

A Rob - yn, gen - til Rob - yn, tell me how thy le - man doth and

Part III

A Rob - yn, gen - til Rob - yn, tell me how thy le - man doth and

* Leman – lover

thow shalt know of myne. A Rob - yn, gen - til Rob-yn,

thow shalt know of myne. A Rob - yn, gen - til Rob-yn,

3 thow shalt know of myne. My la-dy is un-kynde I wis, a-lac why is she so, she

tell me how thy le-man doth and thow shalt know of myne. A Rob - yn,

tell me how thy le - man doth and thow shalt know of myne. A Rob - yn,

9 lov'th an - oth- er bet-ter than me and yet she will say no. A Rob - yn,

gen - til Rob-yn, tell me how thy le - man doth and thow shalt know of myne.

gen - til Rob-yn, tell me how thy le-man doth and thow shalt know of myne.

35 gen - til Rob-yn, tell me how thy le-man doth and thow shalt know of myne. I

8

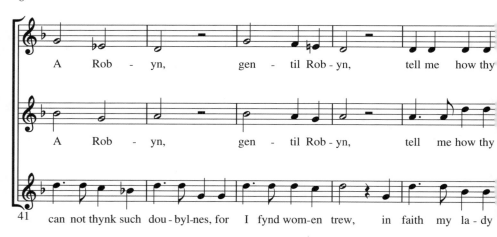

4. BLOW THY HORNE, THOU JOLLY HUNTER

Thomas Ravenscroft
(c1582–c1635)

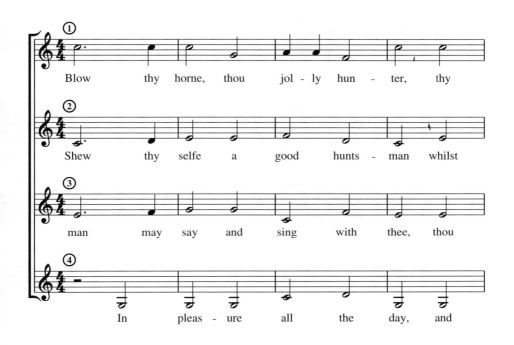

① Blow thy horne, thou jol - ly hun - ter, thy

② Shew thy selfe a good hunts - man whilst

③ man may say and sing with thee, thou

④ In pleas - ure all the day, and

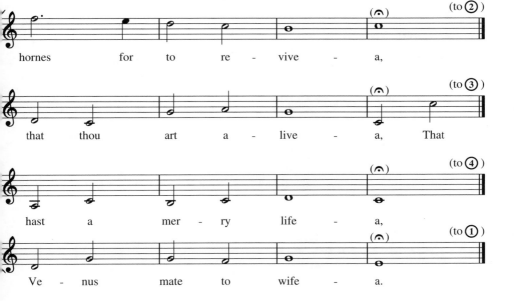

hornes for to re - vive - a, (to ②)

that thou art a - live - a, That (to ③)

hast a mer - ry life - a, (to ④)

Ve - nus mate to wife - a. (to ①)

5. CHRISTMAS IS COMING

English

Christ - mas is com - ing, the goose is get - ting fat,

Please to put a pen - ny in the old man's _ hat,

Please to put a pen - ny in the old man's _ hat.

6. COME FOLLOW

John Hilton (1599–1657)

Come fol - low, fol - low, fol - low, fol - low, fol - low, fol - low me.

Whith-er shall I fol - low, fol - low, fol - low, whith-er shall I fol - low, fol - low thee?

To the green-wood, to the green-wood, to the green-wood, green-wood tree!

7. COME LET US ALL A-MAYING GO

John Hilton (1599–1657)

Come let us all a - may - ing go, and
The bells shall ring - a, the bells shall ring, and the
drums shall beat, the fifes shall play, and

light - ly, and light - ly trip it* to and ___ fro. (to ②)
cuck-oo, ___ the cuck-oo, ___ the cuck-oo ___ sing. The (to ③)
so we'll ___ spend our ___ time a - way. (to ①)

* Trip it – dance

8. DAME, LEND ME A LOAF

Melvill Collection

9. FIE, NAY, PRITHEE, JOHN

Henry Purcell (1659–1695)

* Fie – word of disgust; Prithee – I pray thee; Bout – excess;
Farthing – one quarter of an old (pre-1971) English penny

10. FLOW, O MY TEARS

Anonymous
Based on "Flow, My Tears"
by John Dowland (1600)

Flow, _____ O my tears, Flow, _____ O my tears, Flow, _____ O my tears and cease not.

A - las, these your _____ spring tides!

A - las, a - las, _____ these _ your spring tides in - crease not. O, _____ when?

O, _____ when be - gin you to swell so high that I may drown me in you, that I may drown me in you?

11. FOLLOW ME QUICKLY

Melvill Collection

Fol - low me quick - ly, Jack is a pret - ty boy:

Round a - bout, stand - ing stout, sing - ing all in a boll;*

La la sol la, my dir - rie* come dan - dy.

* Boll – circle; Dirrie – form of "dearie"

12. HE THAT WILL AN ALE-HOUSE KEEP

Anonymous

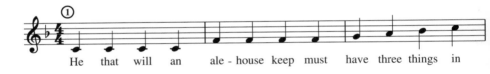

He that will an ale - house keep must have three things in

store: a cham - ber and a feath - er bed, a

chim - ney and a hey no - ny no - ny, hey no - ny no - ny,

hey no - ny no, hey no - ny no, hey __ no - ny no.

13. HARK! THE BONNY CHRISTCHURCH BELLS RING

Anonymous (English)

Hark! The bon - ny Christ - church bells ring: One,

Hark! The first and sec - ond bell, That

Tin - gle, tin - gle, ting, goes the small bell at nine, To

two, three, four, five, six. They sound so won - drous great, so

ev - 'ry day at four and ten cries: "Come, come, come, come,

call the lag - gards* home; But the dev - il a man will

won - drous sweet; And they toll so mer - ri - ly, mer - ri - ly.

come to prayers!" And the ver - ger* trips* be - fore the dean.*

leave his __ can Till he hears the might - y Tom.

(to ②)
(to ③)
(to ①)

* Laggards – those who lag; Verger – official who takes care of the interior of a church;
  Trips – runs or steps lightly; Dean – dignitary in cathedral churches who presides over the chapter

14. HEY DOWN A DOWN

Anonymous

Part III — *(3rd time)* — Hey down a down be - hold and

Part II — *(2nd time)* — Hey down a down be - hold and see

Part I — *(1st time)* — Hey down a down be - hold and see what song is

see what song is this, or how may this be? Three

what song is this or how may this be? Three parts in

this or how may this be? Three parts in one, sing

parts in one, sing af - ter _ me, with hey down down a _

one, sing af - ter _ me, with hey down down a _ down a down,

af - ter _ me, with hey down down a _ down a down, troll the _

down a down, troll the _ ber - ry,* drink and be mer - ry.

repeat ad lib.

troll the _ ber - ry,* drink and be mer - ry.

repeat ad lib.

ber - ry,* drink and be mer - ry.

* Troll the berry – pass 'round the wine

15. HEY HO, ANYBODY HOME?

Old English

Hey ho, an - y - bod - y home? Meat nor drink nor

mon-ey have I none, Yet I will be mer - ry an - y - how. _

16. HEY HO, TO THE GREENWOOD
(Canon)

William Byrd (1543–1623)

19

* Hart – male red-deer; Hind – female red-deer; Roe – small species of European deer (roe-deer)
** Last time, instead of "to the green-," sing "Hey (half note) ho."

17. I GAVE HER CAKES AND I GAVE HER ALE

Henry Purcell (1659–1695)

I gave her cakes and I gave her ale, and I gave her sack* and sher-ry; ____ I kissed her once and I kissed her twice, and we _ were won - d'rous mer-ry. ____ I gave her beads _ and brace-lets fine, and I gave _ her gold _ down der - ry; ____ I thought she was a - feared till she tick - led my beard, and we were won - d'rous mer - ry. ____ Mer-ry we were, mer-ry we were, won-d'rous mer-ry, mer-ry, mer-ry, mer-ry, mer-ry, mer-ry, my hey _ down der - ry; ____ I kissed her once, and I kissed _ her twice, and we were won - d'rous mer-ry. ____

* Sack – old name for a Spanish wine

18. I GOE BEFORE MY DARLING

Thomas Morley (c1557–1602)

* Bowre – bower (shady recess); Wantons – playful persons; Dally – linger

23

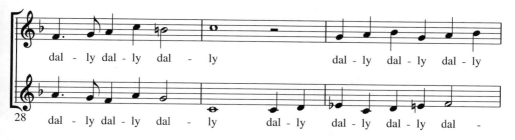

dal - ly dal - ly dal - ly   dal - ly dal - ly dal - ly

dal - ly dal - ly dal - ly   dal - ly dal - ly dal - ly dal -

dal - ly dal - ly dal - ly dal - ly dal - ly.   Ther wee will to -

ly dal - ly dal - ly dal - ly dal - ly.   Ther wee

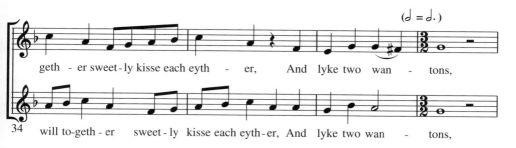

geth - er sweet - ly kisse each eyth - er,   And lyke two wan - tons,

will to - geth - er   sweet - ly kisse each eyth - er,   And lyke two wan - tons,

Dal - ly dal - ly dal - ly dal - ly dal - ly   dal - ly

Dal - ly dal - ly dal - ly dal - ly dal - ly dal - ly dal - ly

dal - ly dal - ly dal - ly dal - ly dal - ly dal - ly dal - ly.

dal - ly dal - ly dal - ly dal - ly dal - ly dal - ly dal - ly.

19. JACK BOY, HO BOY NEWIS

Melvill Book of Roundels

Jack boy, ho boy newis,* The cat is in ye vall.*

Let us ring now for hir knell,* Ding dong, ding dong bell.

* Newis – news; Vall – well; Knell – death toll

20. JOAN, COME KISS ME NOW

English

Joan, come kiss me now, Once a - gain

with thy love gen - tle, Joan, come kiss me now.

21. LADY, COME DOWN AND SEE

Old English

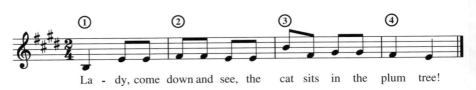

La - dy, come down and see, the cat sits in the plum tree!

22. THE LITTLE BELLS OF WESTMINSTER

English

The lit - tle bells of West-min-ster go Ding! Ding! Ding! Dong! Dong!

23. JOLLY SHEPHERD

Book of Roundels, 1612

Jol - ly shep - herd and up on a hill as he sat, So

loud he blew his lit - tle horn and kept right well his gait.

Ear - ly in a morn - ing late in an eve - ning, And

ev - er blew this lit - tle boy so mer - ri - ly pip - ing.

Ter - li - ter lo, ter - li - ter lo, _____ ter - li - ter lo, ter - li!

Ter - li - ter lo, ter - li - ter lo, ter - li - ter lo, ter - li!

24. LITTLE JACK HORNER

Traditional English

Lit-tle Jack Hor-ner sat in a cor-ner eat-ing his Christ-mas pie. He

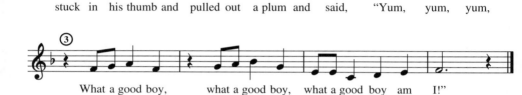

stuck in his thumb and pulled out a plum and said, "Yum, yum, yum,

What a good boy, what a good boy, what a good boy am I!"

25. MUSING

Book of Roundels, 1612

Mus - ing, mus - ing, mus - ing my own self all a - lone, I heard a

maid, I heard a maid, I heard a maid mak - ing great moan, With sobs

and sighs and man - y a griev - ous moan, For that,

for that, for that her maid - en - head was gone. Mus - ing,

* Sing G♯ last time only.

26. MY DAME HATH A LAME, TAME CRANE

Anonymous

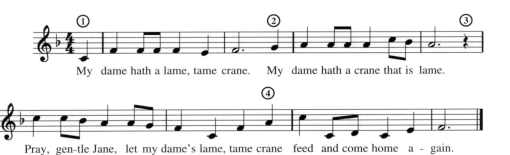

My dame hath a lame, tame crane. My dame hath a crane that is lame.

Pray, gen-tle Jane, let my dame's lame, tame crane feed and come home a - gain.

27. NEW OYSTERS

Thomas Ravenscroft (c1582–c1635)

New oy - sters, new oy -

At a groat* a pecke, at a groat a

Fetch us bread and wine that we may eat, let us lose no time with

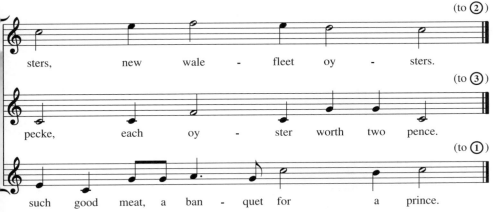

(to ②)

sters, new wale - fleet oy - sters.

(to ③)

pecke, each oy - ster worth two pence.

(to ①)

such good meat, a ban - quet for a prince.

* Groat – a former English coin

28. NOW GOD BE WITH OLD SIMEON

Book of Roundels, 1612

Now God be with old Sim - e - on, for he made cans for

man - y a - one, and a good old man was he. And

Jen - kin was his jour - ney-man, and he could tip - ple* off

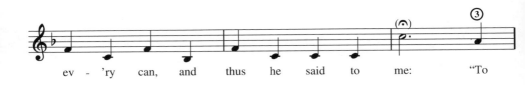

ev - 'ry can, and thus he said to me: "To

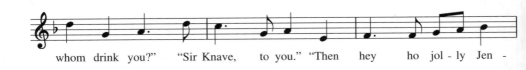

whom drink you?" "Sir Knave, to you." "Then hey ho jol - ly Jen -

kin, I spy a knave in drink - ing. Come pass the bowl to me."

* Tipple – drink often

29. NOW, ROBIN, LEND TO ME THY BOW

Old English

1. Now, Rob-in, lend to me thy bow, Sweet Rob - in, lend to me thy bow, For
2. With that the la - dy she came in, And willed them all for to a-gree; For

I must now a hunt - ing with my la - dy go, With my sweet la - dy go.
hon-est hunt-ing nev - er was ac-count-ed sin, Nor nev - er shall __ for me.

Note: The 1st, 2nd and 3rd parts should repeat part of the 1st verse after finishing the 2nd verse.
A convenient finish will be found when the 1st part reaches the end of the 3rd section.
This enables the 4th part to finish the 2nd verse.

30. OAKEN LEAVES

Thomas Ravenscroft (1609)

Oak - en leaves in the mer - ry wood so wild, when will you grow

green - a? Fair - est maid, and thou be with child,

Lul - la - by may'st thou sing - a. Lul - la lul - la-by,

lul - la lul - la lul - la - by, lul - la - by may'st thou sing - a.

31. ONCE, TWICE, THRICE

Henry Purcell (1659–1695)

* Claret – French light red wine

32. ONE, TWO, THREE, OUR NUMBER IS RIGHT (Catch)

Henry Purcell (1659–1695)

32

33. A ROUND OF THREE COUNTRY DANCES IN ONE

Thomas Ravenscroft (c1582–c1635)

Bass II: Sing af - ter fel - lows as you hear me, a toy that sel - dom is seen - a. Three coun - try danc - es in one to be, a pret - ty con-

Bass I: ceit as I ween* - a. Sing Rob - in Hood, Rob - in Hood, said lit - tle

Bass II: af - ter fel - lows as you hear

John, come dance be - fore the Queen - a. In a red

me, a toy that sel - dom is seen - a. Sing coun - try
(Three)

pet - ti-coat and a green jack - et, a white hose and a ___

danc - es in one to be, a pret - ty con - ceit as

* Ween – think

* Foot it – dance; Swithen – person's name (one of the dancers); Trick it – dance

34

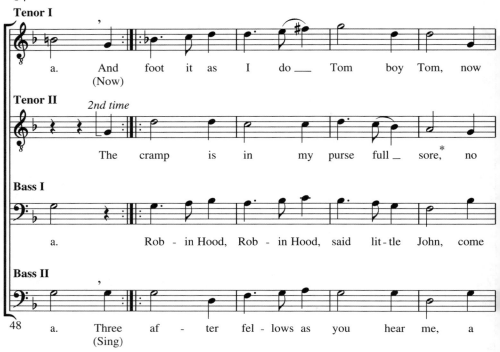

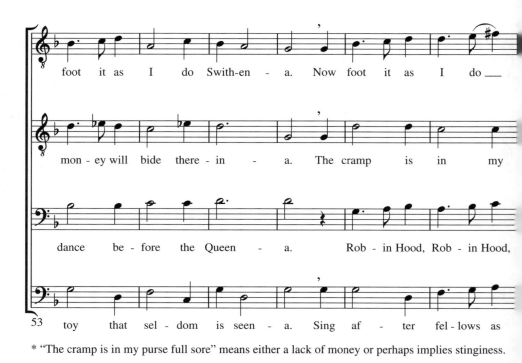

* "The cramp is in my purse full sore" means either a lack of money or perhaps implies stinginess.

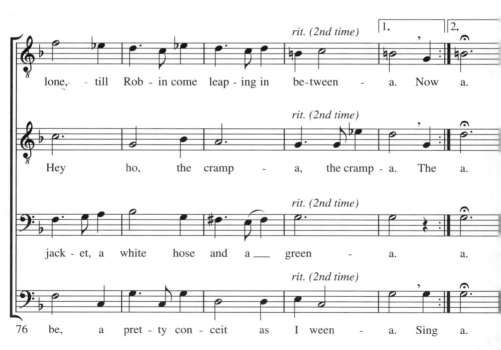

Note: Though written for TTBB voices, this piece could possibly be performed with mixed voices, perhaps even transposing up.

34. THE SILVER SWAN

Orlando Gibbons (1583–1625)

The sil - ver swan, who liv - ing had no

Lean - ing her breast a - gainst the reed - y

"Fare-well, all joys, ___ O ___ death, come close my

(to ②)

note, When death ap-proached un - locked her si - lent throat.

(to ③)

shore, Thus sang ___ her first and last ___ and sang no more:

(to ①)

eyes. More geese than swans now live, more fools than wise!"

35. SINCE TIME SO KIND

Henry Purcell (1659–1695)

* Fie – word of disgust

36. SING WE NOW MERRILY

Book of Roundels, 1612

①
Sing we now mer - ri-ly, our purs - es are emp - ty. Hey

②
ho! Let him take care that lists to spare, for

③
I will not do so. Who can sing so

④
mer-ry a note as he that can-not change a groat!* Hey

⑤
ho, trol - lie lol-lie, trol-lie lol-lie lo!

*Groat – former English coin of small amount

40

37. SING WITH THY MOUTH
Thomas Ravenscroft (c1582–c1635)

Sing with thy mouth, sing with thy heart, like faith-ful friends, sing loath to de - part. Though friends to - geth - er may not al - ways re-main, yet loath to de - part, sing once a - gain.

38. SING YOU NOW AFTER ME
Thomas Ravenscroft (c1582–c1635)

Sing you now af - ter me, and as I sing, sing ye. So shall we well a - gree, five parts in u - ni - ty. Ding, ding a ding a ding a dong bell.

39. SUMMER IS A-COMING IN

Anonymous (ca. 1250)

Notes: The Bass line is to be sung twice before the first part enters, then repeated until the end of the piece. If you have enough low singers, the Basses can divide into two groups – the second group starting at the asterisk. Where marked, the other parts begin singing. You may use as few as 3 parts or as many as 12. You may also choose where and when to stop.

40. TAN TA RA RAN TAN TANT

Thomas Weelkes (1576?–1623?)

* Rampier – rampart? (fortification)

41. THERE WAS AN OLD MAN

Anonymous

There was an old man, an old man who said, "How shall I 'scape from this hor - ri - ble, hor - ri - ble cow? If I sit on a stile, and con - tin - ue to smile, Shall I soft - en the heart, the heart of this cow?"

42. TO PORTSMOUTH

Book of Roundels, 1612

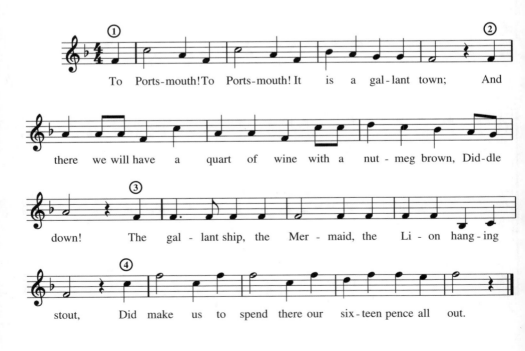

To Ports-mouth! To Ports-mouth! It is a gal - lant town; And there we will have a quart of wine with a nut - meg brown, Did-dle down! The gal - lant ship, the Mer - maid, the Li - on hang - ing stout, Did make us to spend there our six - teen pence all out.

43. TURN AGAIN, WHITTINGTON

Anonymous

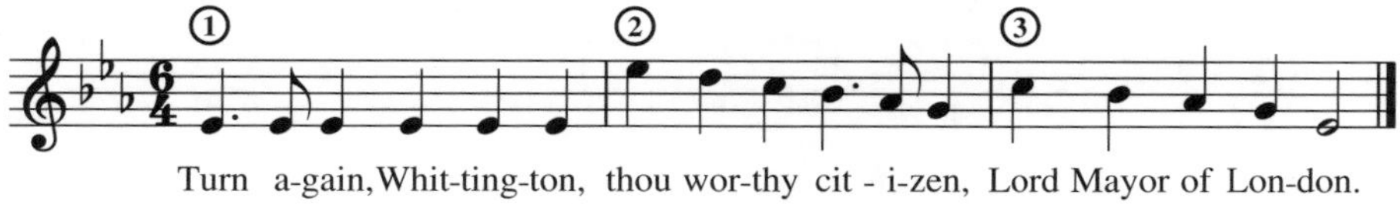
Turn a-gain, Whit-ting-ton, thou wor-thy cit - i-zen, Lord Mayor of Lon-don.

44. UNDER THIS STONE

Henry Purcell (1659–1695)

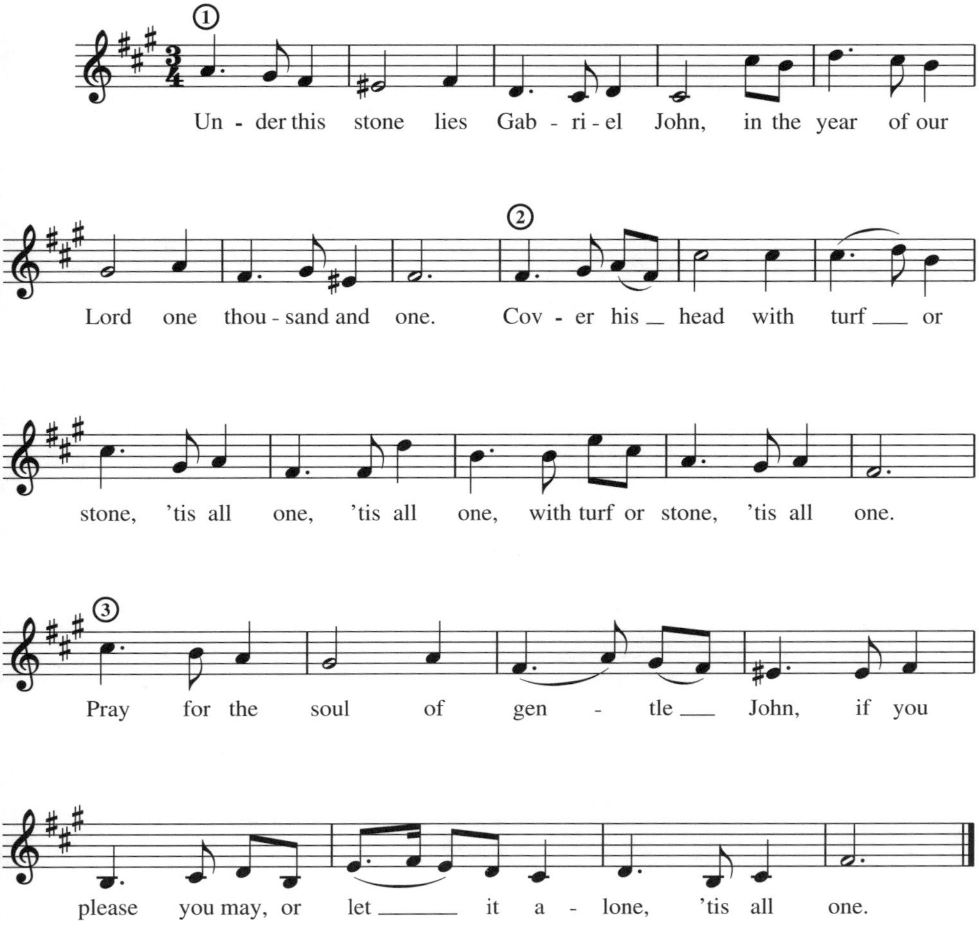
Un - der this stone lies Gab - ri - el John, in the year of our
Lord one thou - sand and one. Cov - er his _ head with turf ___ or
stone, 'tis all one, 'tis all one, with turf or stone, 'tis all one.
Pray for the soul of gen - tle ___ John, if you
please you may, or let ______ it a - lone, 'tis all one.

45. VIVA LA MUSICA
(Long Live Music)

Michael Praetorius (1571–1621)

Vi - va, vi - va la mu - si - ca. Vi - va, vi - va la
mu - si - ca. Vi - va la mu - si - ca!

46. WELL RUNG, TOM, BOY!

English

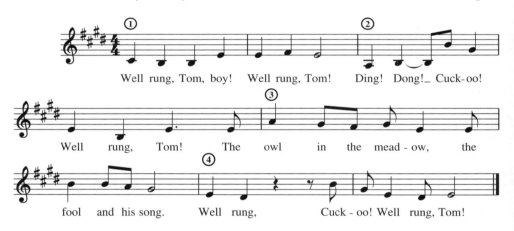

Well rung, Tom, boy! Well rung, Tom! Ding! Dong! Cuck-oo!
Well rung, Tom! The owl in the mead - ow, the
fool and his song. Well rung, Cuck - oo! Well rung, Tom!

47. WHITE CORAL BELLS

English

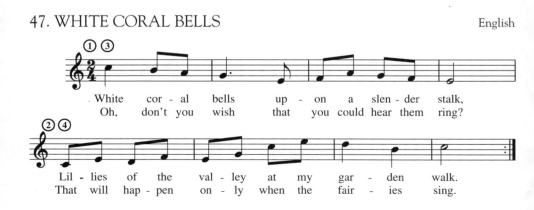

White cor - al bells up - on a slen - der stalk,
Oh, don't you wish that you could hear them ring?
Lil - lies of the val - ley at my gar - den walk.
That will hap - pen on - ly when the fair - ies sing.

48. WHITE SAND AND GREY SAND

Anonymous

White sand and grey sand; Who'll buy my white sand? Who'll buy my grey sand?

49. WHO'LL BUY MY ROSES?

Anonymous

Who'll buy my ros - es? Who'll buy my po - sies? Who'll buy my lil-lies,

lad - ies fair? Taste and try be-fore you buy fine ripe pears.

Taste and try be-fore you buy fine ripe pears. Clothes, clothes,

an - y old clothes for sale or hare skins, rab - bit skins, an - y old clothes.

50. ALLELUYA

French

Al - le - lu - ya, Al - le - lu - ya,

Al - le - lu - ya, Al - le - lu - ya.

51. BENEDICTUS

Adam Gumpelzhaimer (1559–1625)

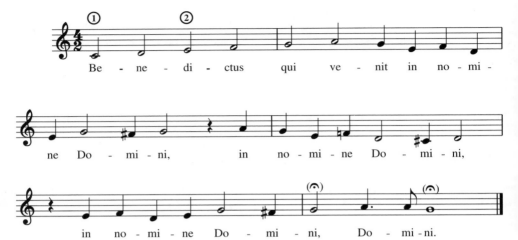

Be - ne - di - ctus qui ve - nit in no - mi -

ne Do - mi - ni, in no - mi - ne Do - mi - ni,

in no - mi - ne Do - mi - ni, Do - mi - ni.

Translation: Blessed is He who comes in the name of the Lord.

52. CHRISTE, DER DU BIST TAG UND LICHT

16th Century

Chri - ste, __ der __ Du bist Tag und Licht, vor Dir ist

Herr, ver - ber - gen nichts; Du Va - ter li - chen __

Lich - tes Glanz, Lehr uns den Weg der Wahr - heit ganz, Wahr - heit ganz.

Translation: Christ, our day and light, You are Lord, from whom nothing is hidden;
As the Father's clear light shines, teach us the way of truth completely.

53. DE TERRA CHRISTUS ASCENDIT

Adam Gumpelzhaimer (1559–1625)

De ter - ra Chri - stus a - scen - dit ad coe - los, qui pri -

us de - scen - de - rat de coe - lo, qui pri - us de - scen - de - rat

de coe - lo, de coe - lo.

Translation: From earth, Christ ascended to heaven, who first descended from heaven.

54. DONA NOBIS PACEM
(Give Us Peace)

Traditional

Do - na no - bis pa - cem, pa - cem. Do - na __

no - bis pa - cem. Do - na

no - bis pa - cem. Do - na no - bis pa -

cem. Do - na no - bis __ pa - cem.

Do - na no - bis pa - cem.

Option: Hum or "oo" last time.

55. HAPPY BE THOU, HEAVENLY QUEEN
(Edi Beo Thu, Hevene Quene)

Anonymous (14th Century)

Hap - py be ___ thou, heav - en - ly Queen, ___
*E - di be - o thu, hev - en - e Quen - e,

Hap - py be thou, heav - en - ly Queen,
*E - di beo thu, hev - en - e Quen - e,

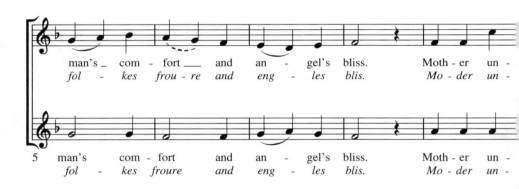

man's __ com - fort ___ and an - gel's bliss. Moth - er un -
fol - kes frou - re and eng - les blis. Mo - der un -

5 man's com - fort and an - gel's bliss. Moth - er un -
fol - kes froure and eng - les blis. Mo - der un -

stain - ed and maid - en clean, ___ such ___ in
wem - med and maid - en cle - ne, swich __ in

10 stain - ed and maid - en clean, such in
wem - med and maid - en cle - ne, swich in

*Original Old English lyrics

56. JESU, REX ADMIRABILIS

Giovanni Pierluigi da Palestrina
(c1525–1594)

Translation: Jesus, wondrous King and noble Victor! Ineffably sweet, wholly desirable!

57. JUBILATE DEO
(Joyfully Sing to God)

Michael Praetorius (1571–1621)

Ju - bi - la - te De - o, Ju - bi - la - te

De - o, Al - le - lu - ia.

58. O LORD, TURNE NOT AWAY THY FACE

Thomas Ravenscroft
(c1582–c1635)

O Lord, turne not a - way Thy face from him that lieth pros - trate,

La - ment - ing sore his sinne - ful life be - fore Thy mer - cies gate,

Which gate Thou op'n - est wide to those that doe la - ment their sinne,

Shut not that gate a-gainst me Lord, but let me en - ter in.

59. NON NOBIS, DOMINE

William Byrd (1543–1623)
Latin Text from Psalm 115

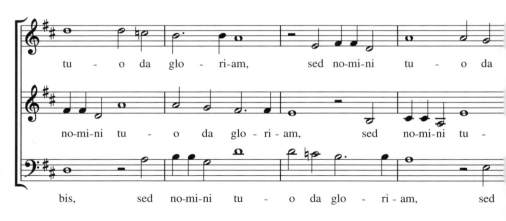

Translation: Not to us, O Lord, not to us, but to Your name give the glory.

60. OH PRAISE THE LORD

Melvill Collection

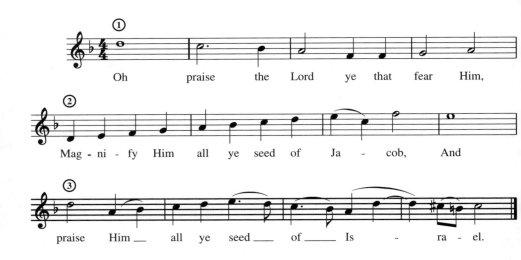

Oh praise the Lord ye that fear Him,

Mag - ni - fy Him all ye seed of Ja - cob, And

praise Him __ all ye seed __ of __ Is - ra - el.

61. TALLIS' CANON

Thomas Tallis (1505–1585)
Words: Bishop T. Ken (1637–1711)

Glo - ry to Thee, my God, this night for all the bless-ings of the light; Keep

me, O keep me, King of Kings, be - neath Thine own al - might - y wings.

Additional Lyrics

2. Forgive me, Lord, for Thy dear Son,
   The ill that I this day have done,
   That with the world, myself and Thee,
   I, ere I sleep, at peace may be.

3. O may my soul on Thee repose,
   And with sweet sleep mine eyelids close,
   Sleep that may me more vig-rous make
   To serve my God when I awake.

62. THERE IS A FLOWER

Melchior Vulpius (c1570–1615)

There is a flow - er spring - ing. From ten - der

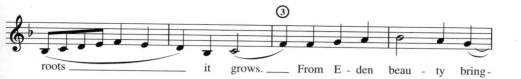

roots _____ it grows. _____ From E - den beau - ty bring -

- ing, from Jes - se's stem, _____ a rose. _____

Note: The tune of this Advent round is based on the hymn "Es ist ein Ros entsprungen" by Michael Praetorius (1571 - 1621).

63. FREU DICH DES LEBENS
(Rejoice in Life)

Ludwig van Beethoven (1770–1827)

Freu dich des Le - bens, freu _____ dich, freu _

_____ dich des Le - bens, des Le - bens, des Le - bens.

64. AVE MARIA
(Hail Mary)

Wolfgang Amadeus Mozart (1756–1791)

A - ve Ma - ri - a, A -

- ve _ Ma - ri - a! A - ve,

A - ve _ Ma - ri - a! A - ve

Ma - ri - a, Ma - ri - a! A - ve,

A - ve Ma - ri - a, A - ve, A - ve!

65. FRIENDS, FORGET THE CARES

Wolfgang Amadeus Mozart
(1756–1791)

Friends, for-get the cares that bore us, come and join the jol-ly

cho-rus, a song of praise to hap-py days, let us be mer-ry one and

all. You sit so id-ly in your plac-es, with gloom-y looks up-on your

fac-es, come on, re-joice and raise your voice to hap-py days a song of

praise, a song of praise. Are you like don-keys far too old to bray? Are you like

don-keys far too old to bray? Sing out! Sing out! Sing out now loud and

strong, laugh and be gay. We toast ro-mance and joy-ous song. May they be with us

all life long. Long live, long live, long live ro-mance and song!

66. IF TURN'D TOPSY TURVY

John Stainer (1892)

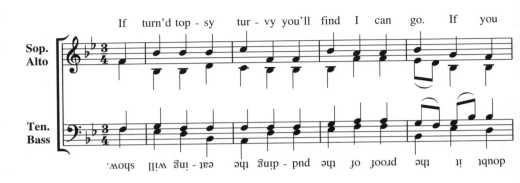

67. I WILL NOT PLEAD

Joseph Haydn (1732–1809)

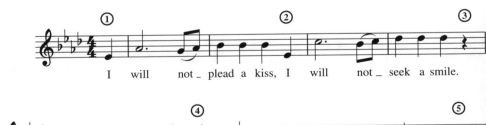

I will not _ plead a kiss, I will not _ seek a smile.

For if I gain a _ kiss you will my heart be-

guile.   A smile would make _ me _ proud, so _ proud the _ while.

68. ALLELUIA

William Boyce (1710–1779)

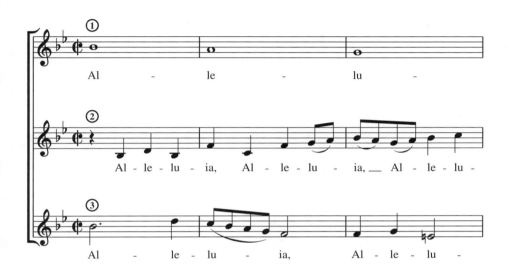

69. WHEN JESUS WEPT

William Billings (1746–1800)

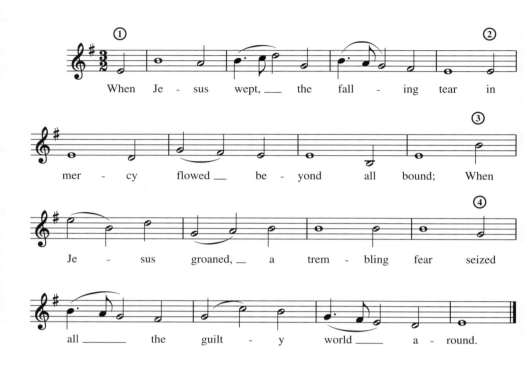

When Je - sus wept, ___ the fall - ing tear in
mer - cy flowed ___ be - yond all bound; When
Je - sus groaned, ___ a trem - bling fear seized
all ___ the guilt - y world ___ a - round.

70. 'TIS THUS, THUS AND THUS

William Boyce (1710–1779)

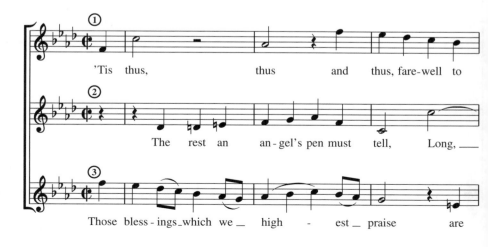

'Tis thus, thus and thus, fare-well to
The rest an an - gel's pen must tell, Long, ___
Those bless - ings_which we _ high - est _ praise are

64

71. COFFEE CANON

Anonymous

C - o - f - f - e - e, Cof - fee is
not _ for _ me. It's a drink some peo - ple wake _ up _ with,
that it makes them ner - vous is _ no _ myth, Slaves to a
cof - fee cup, they can't give cof - fee up.

72. THE NEW DAY

Anonymous

The new day is dawn-ing, let's greet it with danc-ing, The
hills and _ the _ moun-tains with shep - herd _ tunes _ ring - ing. Hey
tu - li tu - li tu - li tu - la, hey tu - li tu - li tu - li ho!

73. WELCOME, WELCOME, EV'RY GUEST
(Canon Four in One)

American *(The Sacred Harp)*

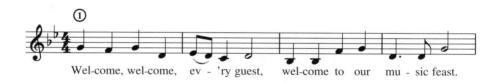

Wel-come, wel-come, ev - 'ry guest, wel-come to our mu - sic feast.

Mu - sic is our on - ly _ cheer, fills both soul and _ rav - ished ear.

Sa - cred muse,_ teach us the mode, sweet-est notes to _ be ex-plored.

Soft - ly swell the trem - bling_ air, to _ com-plete our _ con - cert fair.

74. WAKE UP CANON

American Folk Song

Now all the woods are wak - ing, the sun is ris - ing

high. Wake up now, get up now, be - fore the dew is dry.

75. SWIFTLY FLOWING LABE

Czechoslovakian

A - cross the fields of gold and green A young boy's head is plain - ly seen. A - hu - ya, hu - ya, hu - ya - ya, swift-ly flow-ing La - be,* A - hu - ya, hu - ya, hu - ya - ya, swift-ly flow-ing La - be.

* Labe – Elbe River

76. THE OWL AND THE CUCKOO

Anonymous European

We hear the night owl call - ing from for - est still and dark, While from the tall - est oak tree the cuck - oo an - swers back: Cuck - oo, cuck - oo, cuck - oo, cuck-oo, cuck - oo. Cuck - oo, cuck - oo, cuck - oo, cuck-oo, cuck - oo.

77. FRENCH CATHEDRALS

French

Or - lé - ans, Beau - gen - cy, No - tre Da - me

de Clé - ry, Ven - dô - me, Ven - dô - me.

Note: This round comes from the medieval carillon of Vendôme. It names the French towns that Joan of Arc (known as the Maid of Orléans) was to rescue from the English army during the fifteenth century.

78. ALL THINGS SHALL PERISH
(Music Alone Shall Live)

German

All things shall per - ish from un - der the sky, Mu - sic a - lone shall live,
Him - mel und Er - de müs - sen ver - geh'n, A - ber die Mu - si - ka,

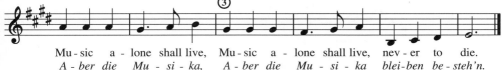

Mu - sic a - lone shall live, Mu - sic a - lone shall live, nev - er to die.
A - ber die Mu - si - ka, A - ber die Mu - si - ka blei - ben be - steh'n.

79. HAVA NA SHIRA

Hebrew

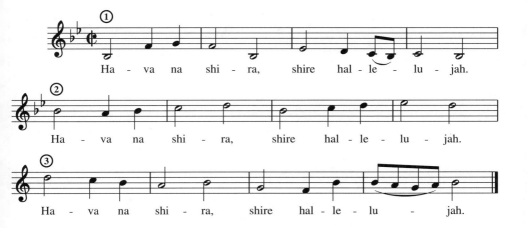

Ha - va na shi - ra, shire hal - le - lu - jah.

Ha - va na shi - ra, shire hal - le - lu - jah.

Ha - va na shi - ra, shire hal - le - lu - jah.

Translation: Come, let us sing a song, Hallelujah.

80. KUKURIKU

Hebrew

A - kum bach - ur   at - zel, ____   ve - tzey   la   a - vo -
da.   A - Kum,   kum, ____   ve - tzey   la   a - vo - da.
Ku - kur - i - ku,   ku - kur - i - ku,   a - tar - ne - gal   ka - ra.

English: Wake up the rooster's crowing, it's time to go to work. *(repeat)*
Wake, wake, it's time to go to work. *(repeat)*
Kukuriku, kukuriku, hear the rooster crow. *(repeat)*

81. LO YISA GOI

Hebrew

Lo yi - sa   goi   el   goi   che - rev,   lo yil - m' - du   od   mil - cha -
ma,   Lo   yi - sa   goi   el   goi   che - rev,   lo   yil - m' -
du   od   mil - cha - ma.   Lo   yi - sa goi   el   goi   che - rev,
lo   yil - m' - du   od   mil - cha - ma,   Lo   yi - sa   goi   el
goi   che - rev,   lo   yil - m' - du   od   mil - cha - ma.

Translation: Nation will not lift up sword against nation, nor will they learn war any more.
(Isaiah 2:4)

82. SHALOM CHAVERIM

Hebrew

Sha - lom cha-ve-rim, sha - lom cha-ve-rim, sha - lom, sha - lom, L' -

hit - ra - ot, l' - hit - ra - ot, sha - lom, sha - lom.

English: Shalom,* my friends, shalom, my friends, shalom, shalom,
We'll see you again, we'll see you again, shalom, shalom.

* Peace

83. PERCHÉ VEZZOSI RAI

Italian

Per-ché vez - zo - si rai ____ tan-to ri - gor per - ché.

Non tro - va - re ____ te mai ____ chi vi ami al _ par di me,

Mai, mai, ma - i chi vi ami al _ par di me.

Translation: Tell me, O charming rays,
Why so much rigor, why?

For you will never find
One who loves you more than I,

Never, never,
One who loves you more than I.

84. HOTARU KOI

Traditional Japanese

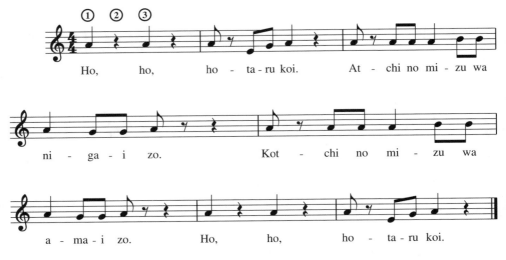

Ho, ho, ho - ta - ru koi. At - chi no mi - zu wa

ni - ga - i zo. Kot - chi no mi - zu wa

a - ma - i zo. Ho, ho, ho - ta - ru koi.

Translation: Come, firefly, come. Over there the water is nasty. Over here the water is sweet.

85. MI GALLO

Mexican

Mi gal-lo se mu - rió a - yer. Ya no can-ta - rá co-co-

rí, co - co - rá, Ya no can - ta - rá co - co - rí, co - co - rá.

Co - co - rí, co - rí, co - co - rí, co - rá.

Translation: My rooster died yesterday. He no longer cries, "Cock-a-doodle doo."

86. ROUND

Ludwig van Beethoven (1770–1827)

Note: The following wordless rounds may be sung on neutral syllables such as "doo," "loo," etc. Or, be creative and make up your own lyrics.

87. ROUND 1

Antonio Caldara (1670–1736)

88. ROUND 2

Antonio Caldara (1670–1736)

89. ROUND 3

Antonio Caldara (1670–1736)

90. ROUND

Christoph Demantius (1567–1643)

91. ROUND

Joseph Haydn (1732–1809)

92. ROUND 1

Wolfgang Amadeus Mozart (1756–1791)

76

93. ROUND 2

Wolfgang Amadeus Mozart (1756–1791)

94. ROUND

Giacomo Antonio Perti (1661–1756)

95. ROUND

Giuseppe Ottavio Pitoni (1657–1743)

96. ROUND

Antonio Salieri (1750–1825)

97. ROUND

Franz Schubert (1797–1828)

98. ROUND

Georg Philipp Telemann (1681–1767)

99. IF TURN'D TOPSY TURVY

John Stainer (1892

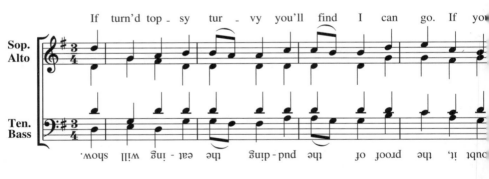

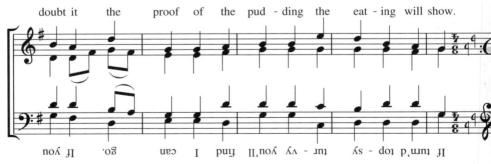